30 Day Leadership Challenge Workbook

Brian J. Ward

WWW.FIREHOUSELEADERSHIP.COM

The recommendations, advice, descriptions and the methods described in this book are presented solely for educational purposes. The author and publisher assume no liability whatsoever for any loss or damage that results from the use of any of the material in this book. Use of the material in this book is solely at the risk of the user.

Author: Brian J. Ward

Reviewers:
Deputy Fire Chief - Operations, Freddie Fernandez, City of Miami Fire Rescue (FL), Retired

Engineer, Tommy Goran, City of Columbia Fire Department (MO)

Lieutenant, Ben Martin, Henrico County Division of Fire (VA)

ISBN-13: 978-1983422874 (paperback), First Edition

Published: March 29, 2019

All rights reserved. No part of this book may be reproduced, stored in a retrieval system or transcribed in any form or by any means, electronic or mechanical, including photocopying and recording, without the prior written permission of the publisher.

Printed in North Charleston, South Carolina
United States of America

Dedication

To my two-year old daughter Belle and my baby boy Tyson. When you read this in 20 years I hope that you will remember to always be your best regardless of the situation and learn every chance you get. If you want it – strive to make your dreams come true.

And, thank you to my wife Brooke for all of your support!

Love Dad

Acknowledgements

I would like to provide a special thank you to the following people for their support and guidance through this project.

Freddie Fernandez – Retired Deputy Chief of Operations, City of Miami (FL) Fire Rescue and Founder of Fire Service Assessment Prep www.fireassessmentcenterprep.com/.

Tommy Goran – Engineer, City of Columbia (MO) Fire Department and Founder of Flashover Leadership. www.flashoverleadership.com.

Ben Martin – Lieutenant, Henrico County (VA) Division of Fire and Founder of Embrace the Resistance. www.embracetheresistance.com

Contents

Preface

Instructions

Day 1: One More Step   10

Day 2: Step Outside Your Industry   12

Day 3: Gain Insight   14

Day 4: Overlearning Theory   16

Day 5: Positive Reinforcement   18

Day 6: Why Should I Trust You?   20

Day 7: Behavioral Modification   22

Day 8: Find Something Right   24

Day 9: Trust Your Gut   26

Day 10: Family   28

Day 11: Facing Adversity   30

Day 12: GRIT   32

Day 13: Team Building   34

Day 14: Sources of Power   36

Day 15: Creating Goals   38

Day 16: Establish a Vision	40
Day 17: Communicate	42
Day 18: Mentoring	44
Day 19: Mentee	46
Day 20: Networking	48
Day 21: Do What Others Don't Expect	50
Day 22: Integrity	52
Day 23: Time Management	54
Day 24: Organization	56
Day 25: Historical Perspective	58
Day 26: Lead by Example	60
Day 27: Demonstrator of Beliefs	62
Day 28: Compassion	64
Day 29: Not Here to Sell Ice Cream	66
Day 30: Don't be Accidently Successful	68
Closing	70
About the Author	71

Preface

Leadership must be a practiced application. Leadership as a verb is much more effective rather than called upon as a noun. I recently sat in a meeting where a suggestion to the group was to be more accountable. This is and never will be an effective approach or method. If we want to be more accountable, we must put actionable items into play and execute. It does not mean we always get it right or that there are no learning opportunities. However, the continuous progression forward develops our capabilities each and every day.

This text is designed to take one concept of leadership at a time and apply it to your current situation. The intent is to provide the leadership concept in its simplest form without the complexity of leadership formulas or complicated explanations and to create an actionable item. This actionable item will be provided in such a manner that does not require funding, political bureaucracy or the approval of anyone. The items provided simply require you to exhibit passion and an overwhelming desire to be a little better each day.

I hope you enjoy this text which is based on my experience leading individuals and organizations with and without formal rank or title. The characteristics listed are by no means the only characteristics of leadership nor is it stated that if you complete the associated action items that you will automatically become a leader. These are characteristics which have resonated with me in the public and private sector, whether leading an engine company or a multi-million-dollar project. It takes effort and experience to fully appreciate all the concepts. In addition, there is never a stopping point where you suddenly have it all figured out. I've worked through these items with practical applications on the floor with people and through academics for several years and I am still a student of learning. However, starting today, these few items will surely put you on the right path.

—Brian J. Ward

Instructions

The instructions are straight-forward and simple. Look at your work schedule and every day that you work read the corresponding characteristic and complete the action item. If you miss one day, there is no problem, simply pick up where you left off. There is no benefit or reward for finishing the action items in the fastest time possible. The reward is changing behaviors and creating a consistent environment by thoroughly delivering quality actionable items.

Once you complete the corresponding action item take the time to write down what action you took. Be sure to provide any valuable information learned or for reference at a later date. Once you complete all 30 action items go back and review the content of what you have learned over the last several weeks. The challenge after you complete this text is to continue your efforts through completing the action items a second time or creating your own action items.

Day 1: One More Step

Consider where you are today by thinking about your abilities, including your knowledge and physical skill sets. What do you wish to be better at? Understanding your own strengths and weaknesses will assist you in this determination. Furthermore, your strengths can drive improvements within the items which you determine are personal weaknesses. A characteristic of great leaders includes not settling for the status quo and determining what is that one more step. Once you have determined the next step, continue looking down the road for the next step and opportunity. Soon this will all become a habit that you no longer consciously think about.

Action Item: Consider where you are today and what may be a weakness or an area of improvement for you personally. What is your next step and how will you achieve it? Take an action today so that you will be better tomorrow.

_____

_____

Day 2: Step Outside Your Industry

Many times, we are indoctrinated by how our organization or industry has always conducted business. Early in our careers this concept may be beneficial if it is properly documented and we have a method of passing on information. However, as we transition from novices to experts in our respective organizations we need to look for continuous improvement. One of the methods of continuous improvement is to look to another organization or industry and learn how they conduct business. For example, being in the fire service I train for subjectively based competency, however, from the private industry I learned to incorporate performance metrics to benchmark my levels of progression even for a skill set such as timing a search. If I only train for competency I am only training to get it right, however, if I am constantly comparing myself against my personal performance metrics I should be able to show marked improvement over time.

Action Item: Select an industry or profession outside of the one you are currently in and research it to understand how they conduct business. Some examples include United States Marine Corps Warfighting Doctrine; Six Sigma in private industry, crew resources management in aviation industry or decision-making capabilities with Dr. Gary Klein.

_____
_____
_____
_____
_____
_____
_____
_____
_____
_____
_____
_____

Day 3: Gain Insight

One of the simplest methods of gaining insight is to spend a few minutes every day reading. It does not necessarily require reading thousands of books which can seem overwhelming if you are not a regular reader. Start by selecting one article today concerning a topic you want to learn more about. You should spend 10 – 15 minutes each day acquiring this knowledge. 10 minutes today may not seem like much, however, multiplied over 365 days you will gain a tremendous amount of insight in various topics, industries and organizations all of which will make you a well-rounded leader.

Action Item: Select a reputable magazine or online article to read for 10-15 minutes and be sure to change the resource every day. Identify a method to share the key points you learned with your team.

_____
_____
_____
_____

Day 4: Overlearning Theory

The overlearning theory states that we should not practice our skills simply to perform them correctly once, however, we should practice until we cannot perform the skill incorrectly. This repetition of skills over and over helps us develop the ability to adapt to any situation we are faced with, even if we have never encountered the situation before. The drive to practice within the overlearning theory transitions us from novices into experts. As we develop to an expert level we are setting the bar higher for those around us without using rank or title, thus increasing the effectiveness of our team. Individuals that operate in a high severity, time constrained occupation apply this theory relentlessly (or at least they should),

Action Item: Whatever skill you will be performing today spend extra time to perform the task in real time at least five additional times. If you have more time attempt 10 additional repetitions.

Day 5: Positive Reinforcement

One of the greatest returns of appreciation I have ever received came from a $5 challenge coin and handing out Gatorades during a tough 100° Georgia summer afternoon. In both situations a simple sign of appreciation gained tremendous respect from those involved. Many times we expect people to perform "because that is their job." However, how many times do we take time away from our "job" without some grand event to positively reinforce behaviors that we want the people around us to exhibit?

Give away items just to say thanks.

Action Item: Find three people (employees or not) doing something correct, even if it's just doing their job and tell them thank you. Soon this will become a habit and something you just do upon seeing the employee or peer action.

Day 6: Why Should I Trust You?

One of the first statements made to me when I assumed responsibility for one of my past organizations during my opening I want to be the best department speeches was "Why should I trust you?" Saying that I was caught off guard would be an understatement. However, it was real and in front of the entire town hall meeting and required a response. Now, the background is that the organization had seen five leaders in three years. Who could they trust? I simply asked for them to give me a chance and communicate with me on what I can do to improve the situation. Once I received the requested items I had to follow through by delivering upon my words. Trust is not given, but gained by the actions you take every day.

Action Item: Take a look at your team today and determine one action you can take to build trust within your team. Maybe it is a positive comment, words of encouragement, or saying yes instead of no. Give your team something that will help them be the best they can be and develop trust with you in the process.

Day 7: Behavioral Modification

Changing behaviors requires one person to establish a mastery level and execute against that level every day. If you want to change the level of performance in your organization it starts with you. Early in my career as an informal leader, another individual and myself established an obstacle course which tested our abilities every shift at the fire house. It required us to wear our complete turnout gear with the self-contained breathing apparatus and required 45 – 60 minutes to complete. Without threats, intimidation or mandates, our entire crew (14 members) joined us every shift. We established what good looked like and the entire team wanted to be a part of it. If you want to change a behavior, be the first to set the bar. Seven years since this assignment and with most of the crew removed, the obstacle course continues to this day because of the culture we established.

Action Item: Create a stretch goal for yourself which will raise the bar for you as an individual and then offer the opportunity for others to join you in your development.

Day 8: Find Something Right

We can always see what someone is doing wrong and as humans we seem to love pointing it out. However, the much more difficult approach is to find someone doing something right. Instead of focusing on disciplinary actions, let's focus on letters of commendation. Once you find this individual don't just tell them thank you, however, this time document the situation, date and time for the employees file. You do not have to be a supervisor to do this. Even if you are a peer and see something right, document it and send it to that person's supervisor to place in the employees file.

Action Item: Find someone doing something right, tell them thanks, document the situation detailing the employee, date, and actions taken. Make sure the document gets into the employee's file, if possible. At a minimum, deliver it to the employee. This can even be done peer to peer.

Day 9: Trust Your Gut

Leaders who have developed expertise through experience and training have the innate ability to make decisions without consciously considering all options. This level of expertise allows the leader to recognize a situation and make the correct decision. This may be closing a business deal in the correct market-based economy or sitting in front of an apartment complex with multiple rooms on fire. Experience comes with time and opportunities. Personal and professional experiences develop an individual.

Action Item: Ask for a stretch assignment or to be a part of a project that is outside of your comfort zone. Even if you must start at the bottom it will provide you with experiences that you can later pull from in future situations. In many situations, you will not remember where you learned specific skill sets, however, the experiences will allow you make decisions by trusting your gut.

Day 10: Family

Regardless of the position or organization I was a part of I always tried to treat the people around me like family. I believe that through developing relationships and treating people respectfully, like family, a bond is created. When the bond is created during calm waters, the bond has something to stand on when times get tough. However, if we have never worked on developing that relationship or bond it is difficult to maintain team integrity and continuity when difficult times arise. Strong teams have common bonds and the common bond is essential to developing a Hi-Performance Team.

Action Item: Spend time today learning something non-work related about your team members. Start the conversation by offering something about you. What are their kid's names? Birthdays? Age? What did the team member do over the weekend? What are their hobbies and interests?

_____

_____

Day 11: Facing Adversity

Any individual attempting to go against the grain or be out front will face adversity and develop a fan base of critics. What if Einstein listened to his school teachers when they said he was a slow learner? What if Emmitt Smith stopped playing football when he was told he was too small? The list goes on and on of individuals who did not let critics stop them. They endured through to the end which makes the success so much sweeter. As a leader, understand that adversity will come but don't let it get you down, stay the course. Leaders exhibit perseverance.

Action Item: Consider an adversity you are facing and write it down. Know that you are not alone in your quest for a better state and that you are paving a way for those coming behind you. Under the adversity you selected, write down all the positives that will come from you staying strong and making a difference. If these items are not for the correct reasons, you may need to adjust your course.

Day 12: GRIT

True leaders have grit. Grit is the ability to persevere when times are tough. It is a non-cognitive and non-physical trait that comes from your heart and passion for the task at hand. People will gravitate towards the individuals who exhibit grit and it lends to your credibility to accomplish missions when it seems impossible. One study from West Point Military Academy suggest that grit is a better indicator of success than academic or physical agility scores. If you are interested in additional information on GRIT, reference Angela Duckworth.

Action Item: Reflect on where you are in life or your career and consider your passion for what you do day in and day out. What drives your passion? Consider your answer and demonstrate it around the people in your life. Passion is contagious.

_____
_____
_____

Day 13: Team Building

Theordroe D. Rossevelt discussed the Man/Woman in the Arena from a critic's standpoint that only those who are in the arena with you are the ones that matter. Those outside of the arena not even attempting to be better or be different, don't matter. However, there is another point which internalizes with me. When we are placed in the arena to fight complacency, mediocrity or adversity as a team a few actions take place. We sweat together, we wipe the same dirt and grime off our faces, and we share the fatigue together. The teams who are placed in these types of situations from experience and training out perform all other teams. By placing ourselves in the arena we show our vulnerabilities, yet we also show our determination and commitment.

Action Item: This action item applies to every day of your life. Never be afraid to jump in the arena and never leave your team in the arena. Whether you are a business professional, firefighter or production line worker show them that you will always be there and you will have their respect forever. Consider a situation that was difficult for your team – how did you handle it? Attempt to recreate a situation that requires the team to work together through a training scenario or simulation.

_____
_____
_____
_____
_____
_____
_____
_____
_____
_____
_____
_____
_____
_____
_____

Day 14: Sources of Power

Leaders develop sources of power through various methods. One of these methods which every individual can obtain on their own is the ability to become an expert. The expert level does not come overnight and no one is entitled to it. However, through asking for the tough assignments, continuous practice, training, education, and creating situations to build experience you can become an expert. Regardless of your title or rank people will notice your actions (cognitive or physical) and they will gravitate towards you. Consider a known expert within your inner circle: why did you just call them an expert without thinking through a hierarchy first? You become a leader by positioning yourself with the knowledge and skill sets that others wish to acquire.

Action Item: Commit to becoming an expert in your given area. Determine what it is you don't know and attack it from a cognitive and physical aspect. If you are unsure how to find the information, you need to ask a mentor or a known expert for that topic even if you have never met that individual. You may be surprised with the response. What are you challenging yourself to be an expert at and what are your steps to achieving?

_____
_____
_____
_____
_____
_____
_____
_____
_____
_____
_____
_____
_____
_____
_____
_____

Day 15: Creating Goals

Leaders have specific goals with results. If you want to be a leader start creating goals. Consider something you want to accomplish and use the SMART format. SMART stands for Specific, Measurable, Attainable, Relevant, and Timely. By using this format, you develop goals which are not ambiguous, it gives you a path, let's you know what success looks like and sets a date to accomplish. I have used this format throughout my life and career to keep me from procrastinating and to create stretch goals for continuous self-improvement. I did not make every goal on time. Life happens, however, attempt to minimize adjusting the dates.

Action Item: Create a SMART Goal today for something you want to accomplish by writing it down and placing it in a place you will see every day. This will also provide visualization which will help you see yourself accomplishing the goal.

_____

_____

Day 16: Establish a Vision

Your team may face internal strife or problems when determining how to tackle an objective and this is normal. A method used by leaders to align team members, regardless of the situation, is to assist them with making tough decisions by establishing a vision. The vision should be built with the entire teams input (creates buy-in) and is communicated so that every individual is clear on the expectations. For example, the U.S. Warfighting Doctrine describes the Commanders Intent as a method of explaining the objective, parameters and outcome needed; however it allows the task performers to make the necessary decisions based on what they encounter.

Action Item: Pull your team together and establish a vision. It should be a clear and concise concept which is understood by all. A vision may only be one to two sentences and it encompass what it means to be a part of a team and it must be remembered. As a fire service leader, I used the Maltese Cross with the eight points of the badge and their definitions as my team's vision.

Day 17: Communicate

The successes and failures of many leaders have been tied to the ability to effectively communicate with their team. As a leader and follower, I always try to listen more than I speak. This allows me to take in everything going on around me and pick up on little intricacies that people are saying but not necessarily telling me. For example, by communicating with my team I can pick up on cultural traits or the current mental state of my team or organization. By picking up on these points, a leader can intervene if needed to clarify a situation or provide additional information. This communication action also let's your team know that you are approachable.

Action Item: Ask your team how they perceive your communication style and effectiveness. Listen to the feedback provided and make adjustments for improvement. Your success comes directly from those supporting you, it helps if they understand that you are approachable and willing to listen.

Day 18: Mentoring

Mentoring should be a focus of every leader. A friend mandated that each of his subordinates be able to discuss in detail three individuals who were not necessarily direct subordinates and how they were being mentored. I commonly ask in many leadership classes for the attendees to name one person that led them to where they are today and then name one person they are actively helping to achieve their dreams. None of us, including myself, would be where we are without a few chances and a little help along the way. One way of developing power within influence is to share the knowledge and skills you possess. The power of influence does not come from rank but from experiences. Having someone to share experiences with can develop all of us.

Pat Wilson and David Rhodes with my daughter Belle – family and mentors.

Action Item: Consider the one person who sticks out in your mind above all as a mentor for you. Now, provide the name of one individual you are actively mentoring to be better. How are you actively mentoring this individual?

_____
_____
_____
_____
_____
_____
_____
_____
_____
_____
_____
_____
_____
_____
_____

Day 19: Mentee

As stated in Day 18, mentoring is a vital part of any leader's success. One of the nuggets of life that I have learned is that you do not wait for someone to mentor you. If you want to be mentored, you position yourself to be mentored, even if it is from people outside your organization. This requires you, as the mentee, to be willing to listen and learn from others. I once had a firefighter, Tommy Goran from Columbia, Missouri, reach out to me, having never met me, for some simple advice. Tommy and I struck up a mutual bond and love for the fire service. I was able to assist Tommy with his first nationally published magazine article. The reciprocal factor of Tommy reaching out to me is that I can also learn from him.

Action Item: Ask a potential mentor a question concerning a topic you want to learn more about. Don't be afraid to start the conversation, even if you have never met them before. You may be surprised and if your first choice does not respond back, move on to the next potential mentor.

_____
_____
_____
_____
_____
_____
_____
_____
_____
_____
_____
_____
_____
_____
_____
_____
_____
_____

Day 20: Networking

Networking is an essential key to reducing the amount of time spent problem solving and program developing. There are very few circumstances where a situation, thought, idea, problem, etc. has not already been encountered by someone else. While each situation may be slightly different the base or root is typically the same as someone in your industry. One of the key characteristics for my career is the ability to produce results in the most efficient manner possible. My current boss stated recently "If I ask you to complete a task, I better watch out how quickly the task is delivered." While it is a nice compliment from my boss, I have no special powers or super intelligent IQ. However, I have built a network and understand how to effectively leverage the network for the task at hand.

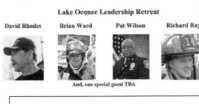

Create your own network opportunity with the Lake Oconee Leadership Retreat.

Action Item: Sign up to attend a conference, seminar, lecture or product demonstration. I always walk away with a new contact who I can call upon with a question. Always have a business card on hand regardless of your title. I will also add that you do not have to be an extrovert type of personality to accomplish this, I'm very much an introvert. However, I understand how to apply my personality for the situation at hand.

Day 21: Do What Others Don't Expect

Leaders do not play by the typical rules and frequently do what others don't expect. One item I have learned is to not pigeon-hole yourself into a stereotype. While there is a military application for the element of surprise, I'm asking you to forget the military concept and think about the people for this moment. Recently, the individual who mentored me as a rookie firefighter, faced a situation where his teenage daughter received a traumatic brain injury from a skateboarding accident.

Knowing the type of individual he is and recently having a daughter myself, all played a part of honoring how he mentored me in the firehouse many years ago. No one would have thought any different for not taking any action, however, I worked with a local custom fire shield leather artist and created a custom, one of a kind, helmet shield that incorporated his fire department, his leadership, his current fire station assignment and his daughter's name.

I left it on the back door of his fire station in an envelope with his name on it. His daughter made a full recovery and now has a custom helmet shield.

Action Item: As I have moved on in the professional sense and don't currently work with the same department no one would have expected anything. However, it meant the world to his family as his daughter made a full recovery after almost a month in the hospital. Your action today is to not forget those who put you where you are and determine a way to make an impact of those outside your direct subordinates. The reciprocal action here is that others take note and start to perform actions that others don't expect. What can you do productive today that no one will expect?

_____
_____
_____
_____
_____

Day 22: Integrity

Integrity is doing what you are supposed to do when no one is looking. In my leadership program, I provide the example of you walking through the employee parking lot and finding a $100 bill with no one else is around. What do you do? Never be the individual to believe you are above doing what is right. This applies even to the point where if you see something that needs immediate attention, then you should take care of the situation. If you are praised for an objective accomplished but it was a team event, be sure to publicly acknowledge the team. This trait also demonstrates to your team that you are willing to "go to bat" or support them when needed.

Action Item: The next time you are praised for the results of an initiative redirect the praise to the individuals who are part of the team. Be specific by calling the individual(s) by name in front of leadership and making it personal. Is there a recent situation where there is still time to provide praise to the team?

Day 23: Time Management

One of the prioritization concerns I hear frequently as reasons for not engaging your team is that there is not enough time. Prioritizing the "must complete" task(s) into buckets will give you time back which can be spent where it counts – with your team.

Action Item: Place the task(s) you must complete today or this week into the following buckets:

Immediate – Handle now and only touch one time. An email needing reply, do not click on in the morning and then again in the afternoon.

Delay – Very low importance or extended due date. Determine when it is due and prioritize based on the need. Do not procrastinate once the date is set.

Long-Term – Long Term is a relevant term depending on the task(s). For these items, plan accordingly so the task(s) is completed in sections or chunks over time and not the whole program the week it is due.

Delete – These task(s) create zero value and should be deleted. What are the items we have done for 100 years that are obsolete? Delete it. The spam email telling you about the latest widget – delete it.

Day 24: Organization

Many times, the simple organization of your camp determines your ability to lead. It has been said that if your camp (office, home, etc..) is in chaos, your leadership capabilities may be in chaos. This does not mean from time to time your truck receives some dirt or that you can't see the bottom of your desk. However, individuals who organized these tangible items generally operate with greater efficiency and it improves their time management.

Action Item: Tackle the dis-organization that you have been avoiding. If it is your desk – file, trash, or complete the task. If it is your calendar – delete what is not important and give yourself space between appointments to catch up. If it is your vehicle or apparatus – pull all equipment off, clean it and put back in the proper space. As Admiral William McRaven said during the University of Texas commencement speech concerning making your bed, "Making your bed provides you with the first accomplishment for the day and gives you the motivation to accomplish the next task." What did you organize today?

Day 25: Historical Perspective

Leaders understand the historical perspectives of their craft and their organization. This allows you to pass on vital information that can be lost and avoid duplicate work (time management) which wastes valuable time repeating task(s) we should have learned from 5, 10, or 15 years ago. There are also valuable lessons connecting the dots as to why we perform task(s) in the method which we do. Leaders should advocate for innovation and experimentation; however, we do not need to spend time repeating failures we should have learned from before.

Jersey City Fire Department Station 2 – Picture depicts the horse and steam engine from station opening

Action Item: Spend time today researching your job duties or responsibilities. When and where did they start? How was it started? Are you currently using a business model that has failed another company? Do you have a similar construction type in your territory to a major incident where numerous firefighters died in collapse situations? Whatever information you learn from your experiences today, be sure to pass the knowledge along and document it so that a line of progression can be shown.

Day 26: Lead by Example

If you are willing to make your employees perform the task, be willing to perform the task yourself. Whether it is moping the floor, typing a memo or carrying yourself in a professional manner. Perform in a manner which you want others to perform. Too many leaders have fallen into say one thing and do another. This is not the example any of us can live by and avoid being a toxic leader. Achieve your credibility through leading by example.

Action Item: Find a task that you normally don't perform and either complete it on your own or at least assist completing the task. Someone cleans your office – you do it, you work at a firehouse and kitchen duties are needed – you do the dishes, or if you want to increase the level of professionalism of your organization – it starts with you acting professional. What task(s) did you complete?

_____

_____

Day 27: Demonstrator of Beliefs

Similar to leading by example, we have to be demonstrators of beliefs. There may be many task(s) that we find tedious, difficult or we practice the "it won't happen to me" mentality. Regardless of the item, we still believe others should perform the task(s). For example, an organization with drivers should always wear their seat belt as it will protect them during an accident and is a good policy. Ask yourself, what happens the first time an employee witnesses you not wearing your seat belt? Credibility is lost. Be a demonstrator of beliefs regardless of how mundane, tedious or difficult the task may be. In your organization, what is that mundane task which leads itself to short cutting and complacency?

Action Item: What is the one item or task that you mandate everyone else to do because it is the right thing to do? However, you have not been living up to the standard which you set. Pick up the task today and start performing. Maybe you currently perform the task but how can you be better at it? How can you demonstrate "want to" versus "having to?"

Day 28: Compassion

Life can be tough in the personal and professional sense. Sometimes employees just need to be shown some compassion and listened too. Compassion shows that you are approachable and willing take time out of your day to help someone on your team. None of us know everything our team members are going through, so before you criticize or reprimand be sure to give the appropriate amount of compassion. It is important to point out that providing compassion should not be confused with having a lack of accountability.

Action Item: The next opportunity where someone exhibits a tough moment or bad day, be available to just listen. Maybe you start off the conversation because you can tell your team member is not their normal self. You do not have to have all the answers and definitely don't make up answers, but offer the assistance. The compassion you provide today will create a team bond that is unbreakable and provides dividends later.

Day 29: Not Here to Sell Ice Cream

Leadership can be tough and sometimes you lose friends who cannot accept the fact that they have to be accountable for themselves. As a teenager, right out of high school my brother once told a group of employees (including me) that if we truly respected him as a person they would never create a situation that made him carry out his formal leadership duties. This thought has stuck with me 20+ years later. A leader cannot be seen as choosing sides or demonstrating bias. A leader must be accountable to the entire team even if that means losing friends and not letting people slide from their responsibilities. In essence, if you would rather keep the friends and not have to make the tough decisions – it may be best to sell ice cream.

Action Item: Use introspection and scan back through some previous decisions you have made regarding your team. Were the decisions fair and were you up to the challenge of holding personnel accountable? If you find a flaw in any of the previous decisions, go address the situation. What items are lurking? Write out how you plan to handle the situation and review your answer tomorrow.

_____
_____
_____
_____
_____
_____
_____
_____
_____
_____
_____
_____
_____
_____
_____
_____
_____
_____
_____
_____

Day 30: Don't be Accidently Successful

We all get lucky from time to time and some even live by the mantra that they would rather be lucky than good. While it is fun to say, there's not much merit to being lucky. As the gambler's fallacy goes, they believe the bad luck will not hit them today. However, as the casino says, the house always wins. We must prepare through training, continuing education, reading, observing, practicing and getting outside of our comfort zone everyday if we are going to avoid falling into the trap of being accidently successful. Leaders do not wait for their dreams to fall into their laps – they seek it out and grab ahold. The first habit from Stephen Covey's Habits of Highly Successful people is being proactive.

Action Item: What do you want to accomplish next week or next year? And, what are you doing to ensure it is achieved? In the fire department, "hoping" to make the right decision as the officer is not a tactic I where I wish to be involved. Don't hope for the next successful project or promotion, put the work in to "know" it will be a success. What area of your profession do you need to be more proactive with and what behaviors are you going to change?

_____
_____
_____
_____
_____
_____
_____
_____
_____
_____
_____
_____
_____
_____
_____
_____
_____
_____

Closing

Thank you for taking the time to read the materials and participate by writing your responses. The next step is to review your answers and see what you learned from this 30-day exercise. We all have areas of improvement we should be working towards. Leadership does not require special powers, it's about people and your interactions with them. It's about developing yourself, so others can learn from you and mimic your behaviors – behavioral modification and leading by example. Your next challenge is to create a positive habit of the items you learned and do not stop the process.

If you have room in the blank spaces repeat this 30-day challenge, write your response and continue to review what you have learned every 30 days. If you are completing this task, with or without this book, you are practicing leadership.

About the Author

Brian J. Ward

BRIAN WARD, CFPS, CEM – Global Emergency Preparedness and Response Leader, Georgia Pacific.

Brian has served as the International Society of Fire Service Instructors (ISFSI) Director At Large and as a member of their Executive Board. He was instrumental in the delivery of the ISFSI 1403 Live Fire Credentialing Program and Vice-Chair since inception; a member of the Principles of Modern Fire Attack Instructor Cadre; and Program Manager for the ISFSI Training Officer's Credentialing Program.

He has authored over 35 nationally publicized articles and research papers, including the Jones and Bartlett Training Officer's Desk Reference and Barn Boss Leadership for the fire service. Brian frequently speaks across North America on leadership, team building, training, and emergency response topics, and is a classroom and workshop instructor for FDIC. He received his Bachelor's Degree in Fire Safety and Technology Engineering from the University of Cincinnati and holds a Master's of Organizational Leadership from Columbia Southern University.

His honors include Fire Department Management from National Association of Counties; Distinguished Service Award, Firefighter of the Year, Top 20 CTBS Instructor and National Seal of Excellence for Leadership and Safety from the National Fallen Fighters Foundation; several ISFSI Organizational Awards; and the ISFSI Presidential Award in 2016. He has served as a member of the Honeywell First Responder Advisory Council, the AFG Criteria Development Committee, Chairman of the Metro Atlanta Training Officers Association and is Certified Georgia Smoke Diver #741.

Made in the USA
Monee, IL
24 December 2021